Laura H

St. Andrew's Episcopal Church

3700 Woodmont Blvd.

Nashville TN 37215

292-9935

D1625411

A Time to Pray

Prayers, Psalms,
and Readings for
Personal Devotions

compiled by
George T. Cobbett

The Church Hymnal Corporation
800 Second Avenue, New York, NY 10017

ISBN 0-89869-073-0

10   9   8   7

Contents

Preface

This book of personal devotions is intended for those who may have only short periods of time each day for prayer and Bible reading. It includes Daily Devotions for Individuals and Families, An Order of Service for Noonday, An Order of Worship for the Evening, and An Order for Compline all from *The Book of Common Prayer*. These devotions follow the basic structure of the Offices of Daily Morning and Evening Prayer by incorporating psalms, scripture and collects or prayers.

The Reconciliation of a Penitent is included for those who might want to use it as part of their personal devotional life.

Members of the Church have expressed a need for a pocket-size book of prayers and readings for personal use based on texts from *The Book of Common Prayer.* The texts included in this edition are in response to expressions of need, and it is hoped they may prove to be of assistance in personal devotion.

The texts of the psalms are from *The Book of Common Prayer,* and the prayers are from the same source and also from *Prayers, Thanksgivings and Litanies* (1973). The twenty-one biblical selections are from *The Common Bible* (Revised Standard Version, an Ecumenical Edition, 1973).

Daily
Devotions

Concerning the Service

These devotions follow the basic structure of the Daily Office of the Church.

When more than one person is present, the Reading and the Collect should be read by one person, and the other parts said in unison, or in some other convenient manner.

For convenience, appropriate Psalms, Readings, and Collects are provided in each service. When desired, however, the Collect of the Day, or any of the Collects appointed in the Daily Offices, may be used instead.

The Psalms and Readings may be replaced by those appointed in

a) the Lectionary for Sundays, Holy Days, the Common of Saints, and Various Occasions.

b) the Daily Office Lectionary.

c) some other manual of devotion which provides daily selections for the Church Year.

Daily Devotions for Individuals and Families

In the Morning

From Psalm 51

Open my lips, O Lord, *
   and my mouth shall proclaim your praise.
Create in me a clean heart, O God, *
   and renew a right spirit within me.
Cast me not away from your presence *
   and take not your holy Spirit from me.
Give me the joy of your saving help again *
   and sustain me with your bountiful Spirit.
Glory to the Father, and to the Son,
     and to the Holy Spirit: *
   as it was in the beginning, is now,
     and will be for ever. Amen.

A Reading

The following or other selection from Holy Scripture

Blessed be the God and Father of our Lord Jesus
Christ! By his great mercy we have been born
anew to a living hope through the resurrection
of Jesus Christ from the dead.   *1 Peter 1:3*

A period of silence may follow.

A hymn or canticle may be used;
the Apostles' Creed may be said.

Prayers may be offered for ourselves and others.

The Lord's Prayer

The Collect

Lord God, almighty and everlasting Father, you
have brought us in safety to this new day: Preserve us with your mighty power, that we may
not fall into sin, nor be overcome by adversity;
and in all we do, direct us to the fulfilling of
your purpose; through Jesus Christ our Lord.
Amen.

At Noon

From Psalm 113

Give praise, you servants of the LORD; *
    praise the Name of the LORD.
Let the Name of the LORD be blessed, *
    from this time forth for evermore.
From the rising of the sun to its going down *
    let the Name of the LORD be praised.
The LORD is high above all nations, *
    and his glory above the heavens.

A Reading

O God, you will keep in perfect peace those whose minds are fixed on you; for in returning and rest we shall be saved; in quietness and trust shall be our strength.   *Isaiah 26:3; 30:14*

Prayers may be offered for ourselves and others.

The Lord's Prayer

The Collect

Blessed Savior, at this hour you hung upon the cross, stretching out your loving arms: Grant that all the peoples of the earth may look to you and be saved; for your mercies' sake. *Amen.*

or this

Lord Jesus Christ, you said to your apostles, "Peace I give to you; my own peace I leave with you:" Regard not our sins, but the faith of your Church, and give to us the peace and unity of that heavenly City, where with the Father and the Holy Spirit you live and reign, now and for ever. *Amen.*

In the Early Evening

This devotion may be used before or after the evening meal. The Order of Worship for the Evening, may be used instead.

O gracious Light,
pure brightness of the everliving Father in heaven,
O Jesus Christ, holy and blessed!

Now as we come to the setting of the sun,
and our eyes behold the vesper light,
we sing your praises O God: Father, Son,
    and Holy Spirit.

You are worthy at all times to be praised
    by happy voices,
O Son of God, O Giver of life,
and to be glorified through all the worlds.

A Reading

It is not ourselves that we proclaim; we proclaim Christ Jesus as Lord, and ourselves as
your servants, for Jesus' sake. For the same God
who said, "Out of darkness let light shine," has
caused his light to shine within us, to give the
light of revelation—the revelation of the glory
of God in the face of Jesus Christ.

2 Corinthians 4:5-6

Prayers may be offered for ourselves and others.

The Lord's Prayer

The Collect

Lord Jesus, stay with us, for evening is at hand and the day is past; be our companion in the way, kindle our hearts, and awaken hope, that we may know you as you are revealed in Scripture and the breaking of bread. Grant this for the sake of your love. *Amen.*

At the Close of Day

Psalm 134

Behold now, bless the LORD,
 all you servants of the LORD, *
 you that stand by night in the
 house of the LORD.
Lift up your hands in the holy place
 and bless the LORD; *
 the LORD who made heaven and earth
 bless you out of Zion.

A Reading

Lord, you are in the midst of us and we are

called by your Name: Do not forsake us, O
Lord our God.   *Jeremiah 14:9,22*

The following may be said

Lord, you now have set your servant free *
    to go in peace as you have promised;
For these eyes of mine have seen the Savior, *
    whom you have prepared for all the world to see
A Light to enlighten the nations, *
    and the glory of your people Israel.

*Prayers for ourselves and others may follow. It is
appropriate that prayers of thanksgiving for the blessings
of the day, and penitence for our sins, be included.*

The Lord's Prayer

The Collect

Visit this place, O Lord, and drive far from it all
snares of the enemy; let your holy angels dwell
with us to preserve us in peace; and let your
blessing be upon us always; through Jesus
Christ our Lord. *Amen.*

The almighty and merciful Lord, Father, Son,
and Holy Spirit, bless us and keep us. *Amen.*

Noonday

An Order of Service for Noonday

Officiant   O God, make speed to save us.
People   O Lord, make haste to help us.

Officiant and People

Glory to the Father, and to the Son, and to the Holy Spirit: as it was in the beginning, is now, and will be for ever. Amen.

Except in Lent, add   Alleluia

A suitable hymn may be sung.

One or more of the following Psalms is sung or said. Other suitable selections include Psalms 19,67, one or more sections of Psalm 119, or a selection from Psalms 120 through 133.

Psalm 119 *Lucerna pedibus meis*

105 Your word is a lantern to my feet *
  and a light upon my path.

106 I have sworn and am determined *
  to keep your righteous judgments.

107 I am deeply troubled; *
  preserve my life, O LORD, according
  to your word.

108 Accept, O LORD, the willing tribute of my lips, *
  and teach me your judgments.

109 My life is always in my hand, *
  yet I do not forget your law.

110 The wicked have set a trap for me, *
  but I have not strayed from your
  commandments.

111 Your decrees are my inheritance for ever; *
  truly, they are the joy of my heart.

112 I have applied my heart to fulfill your statutes *
  for ever and to the end.

Psalm 121   *Levavi oculos*

1   I lift up my eyes to the hills; *
        from where is my help to come?

2   My help comes from the LORD, *
        the maker of heaven and earth.

3   He will not let your foot be moved *
        and he who watches over you will not
            fall asleep.

4   Behold, he who keeps watch over Israel *
        shall neither slumber nor sleep;

5   The LORD himself watches over you; *
        the LORD is your shade at your right hand,

6   So that the sun shall not strike you by day, *
        nor the moon by night.

7   The LORD shall preserve you from all evil; *
        it is he who shall keep you safe.

8   The LORD shall watch over your going out and
            your coming in, *
        from this time forth for evermore.

Psalm 126 *In convertendo*

1 When the LORD restored the fortunes of Zion, *
    then were we like those who dream.

2 Then was our mouth filled with laughter, *
    and our tongue with shouts of joy.

3 Then they said among the nations, *
    "The LORD has done great things for them."

4 The LORD has done great things for us, *
    and we are glad indeed.

5 Restore our fortunes, O LORD, *
    like the watercourses of the Negev.

6 Those who sowed with tears *
    will reap with songs of joy.

7 Those who go out weeping, carrying the seed, *
    will come again with joy, shouldering
        their sheaves.

At the end of the Psalms is sung or said

Glory to the Father, and to the Son, and to
    the Holy Spirit: *
    as it was in the beginning, is now, and will be
        for ever. Amen.

One of the following, or some other suitable passage of Scripture, is read

The love of God has been poured into our hearts through the Holy Spirit that has been given to us. *Romans 5:5*

People   Thanks be to God.

or this

If anyone is in Christ he is a new creation; the old has passed away, behold the new has come. All this is from God, who through Christ reconciled us to himself and gave us the ministry of reconciliation. *2 Corinthians 5:17-18*

People   Thanks be to God.

or this

From the rising of the sun to its setting my Name shall be great among the nations, and in every place incense shall be offered to my Name, and a pure offering; for my Name shall be great among the nations, says the Lord of Hosts. *Malachi 1:11*

People   Thanks be to God.

A meditation, silent or spoken, may follow.

The Officiant then begins the Prayers

Lord, have mercy.
Christ have mercy.
Lord, have mercy.

Officiant and People

Our Father, who art in heaven,
   hallowed be thy Name,
   thy kingdom come,
   thy will be done,
     on earth as it is in heaven.
Give us this day our daily bread.
And forgive us our trespasses,
   as we forgive those
     who trespass against us.
And lead us not into temptation,
   but deliver us from evil.

or the following

Our Father in heaven,
   hallowed be your Name,
   your kingdom come,
   your will be done,
      on earth as in heaven.
Give us today our daily bread.
Forgive us our sins
   as we forgive those
      who sin against us.
Save us from the time of trial,
   and deliver us from evil.

Officiant	Lord, hear our prayer;
People	And let our cry come to you.
Officiant	Let us pray.

*The Officiant then says one of the following Collects.
If desired, the Collect of the Day may be used.*

Heavenly Father, send your Holy Spirit into our
hearts, to direct and rule us according to your
will, to comfort us in all our afflictions, to defend us from all error, and to lead us into all
truth; through Jesus Christ our Lord. *Amen.*

Blessed Savior, at this hour you hung upon the cross, stretching out your loving arms: Grant that all the peoples of the earth may look to you and be saved; for your tender mercies' sake. *Amen.*

Almighty Savior, who at noonday called your servant Saint Paul to be an apostle to the Gentiles: We pray you to illumine the world with the radiance of your glory, that all nations may come and worship you; for you live and reign for ever and ever. *Amen.*

Lord Jesus Christ, you said to your apostles, "Peace I give to you; my own peace I leave with you:" Regard not our sins, but the faith of your Church, and give to us the peace and unity of that heavenly City, where with the Father and the Holy Spirit you live and reign, now and for ever. *Amen.*

Free intercessions may be offered.

The service concludes as follows

Officiant Let us bless the Lord.
People   Thanks be to God.

Evening

Concerning the Service

This Order provides a form of evening service or vespers for use on suitable occasions in the late afternoon or evening. It may be used as a complete rite in place of Evening Prayer, or as the introduction to Evening Prayer or some other service, or as the prelude to an evening meal or other activity. It is appropriate also for use in private houses.

Any part or parts of this service may be led by lay persons. A priest or deacon, when presiding, should read the Prayer for Light, and the Blessing or Dismissal at the end. The bishop, when present, should give the Blessing.

This order is not appropriate for use on Monday, Tuesday, or Wednesday in Holy Week, or on Good Friday. Easter Eve has its own form for the Lighting of the Paschal Candle.

For the Short Lesson at the beginning of the service, any one of the following is also appropriate, especially for the seasons suggested:

Isaiah 60:19-20 (Advent)
Luke 12:35-37 (Advent)
John 1:1-5 (Christmas)
Isaiah 60:1-3 (Epiphany)
1 John 1:5-7 (Lent)
John 12:35-36 (Lent)
Revelation 21:10, 22-24 (Easter)
Psalm 36:5-9 (Ascension)
Joel 2:28-30 (Whitsunday)
Colossians 1:9, 11-14 (Saints' Days)
1 Peter 2:9 (Saints' Days)
Revelation 22:1, 4-5 (Saints' Days)

Any of the prayers in contemporary language may be adapted to traditional language by changing the pronouns and the corresponding verbs.

An Order of Worship for the Evening

The church is dark, or partially so, when the service is to begin.

All stand, and the Officiant greets the people with these words

Light and peace, in Jesus Christ our Lord.

People   Thanks be to God.

In place of the above, from Easter Day through the Day of Pentecost

Officiant   Alleluia. Christ is risen.

People   The Lord is risen indeed. Alleluia.

In Lent and on other penitential occasions

Officiant   Bless the Lord who forgives all our sins;

People   His mercy endures for ever.

One of the following, or some other Short Lesson of Scripture appropriate to the occasion or to the season, may then be read

Jesus said, "You are the light of the world. A city built on a hill cannot be hid. No one lights a lamp to put it under a bucket, but on a lamp-stand where it gives light for everyone in the house. And you, like the lamp, must shed light among your fellow men, so that they may see the good you do, and give glory to your Father in heaven."   *Matthew 5:14-16*

It is not ourselves that we proclaim; we proclaim Christ Jesus as Lord, and ourselves as your servants, for Jesus' sake. For the same God who said, "Out of darkness let light shine," has caused his light to shine within us, to give the light of revelation—of the glory of God in the face of Jesus Christ.   *2 Corinthians 4:5-6*

If I say, "Surely the darkness will cover me, and the light around me turn to night," darkness is not dark to you, O Lord; the night is as bright as the day; darkness and light to you are both alike.   *Psalm 139:10-11*

The Officiant then says the Prayer for Light, using any one of the following or some other suitable prayer, first saying

Let us pray.

Almighty God, we give you thanks for surrounding us, as daylight fades, with the brightness of the vesper light; and we implore you of your great mercy that, as you enfold us with the radiance of this light, so you would shine into our hearts the brightness of your Holy Spirit; through Jesus Christ our Lord. *Amen.*

Grant us, Lord, the lamp of charity which never fails, that it may burn in us and shed its light on those around us, and that by its brightness we may have a vision of that holy City, where dwells the true and never-failing Light, Jesus Christ our Lord. *Amen.*

O Lord God Almighty, as you have taught us to call the evening, the morning, and the noonday one day; and have made the sun to know its going down: Dispel the darkness of our hearts, that by your brightness we may know you to be the true God and eternal light, living and reigning for ever and ever. *Amen.*

Lighten our darkness, we beseech thee, O Lord; and by thy great mercy defend us from all perils and dangers of this night; for the love of thy only Son, our Savior, Jesus Christ. *Amen.*

Advent

Collect for the First Sunday of Advent

Christmas, Epiphany, and other Feasts of the Incarnation

Collect for the First Sunday after Christmas

Lent and other times of penitence

Almighty and most merciful God, kindle within us the fire of love, that by its cleansing flame we may be purged of all our sins and made worthy to worship you in spirit and in truth; through Jesus Christ our Lord. *Amen.*

Easter Season

Eternal God, who led your ancient people into freedom by a pillar of cloud by day and a pillar of fire by night: Grant that we who walk in the light of your presence may rejoice in the liberty of the children of God; through Jesus Christ our Lord. *Amen.*

Festivals of Saints

Lord Christ, your saints have been the lights of the world in every generation: Grant that we who follow in their footsteps may be made worthy to enter with them into that heavenly country where you live and reign for ever and ever. *Amen.*

The candles at the Altar are now lighted, as are other candles and lamps as may be convenient.

During the candle-lighting, an appropriate anthem or psalm may be sung, or silence kept.

The following hymn, or a metrical version of it, or some other hymn, is then sung

O Gracious Light   *Phos hilaron*

O gracious Light,
pure brightness of the everliving Father in heaven,
O Jesus Christ, holy and blessed!

Now as we come to the setting of the sun,
and our eyes behold the vesper light,
we sing your praises, O God: Father, Son,
        and Holy Spirit.

You are worthy at all times to be praised
        by happy voices,
O Son of God, O Giver of life,
and to be glorified through all the worlds.

*The service may then continue in any of
the following ways:*

*With Evening Prayer, beginning with the Psalms;
or with some other Office or Devotion;*

*With the celebration of the Holy Eucharist,
beginning with the Salutation and Collect of the Day;*

*Or, it may be followed by a meal or other activity,
in which case Phos hilaron may be followed by the
Lord's Prayer and a grace or blessing;*

*Or, it may continue as a complete evening Office
with the following elements:*

Selection from the Psalter. Silence, or a suitable Collect, or both, may follow the Psalmody.

Bible Reading. A sermon or homily, a passage from Christian literature, or a brief silence, may follow the Reading.

Canticle. The Magnificat or other canticle, or some other hymn of praise.

Prayers. A litany, or other suitable devotions, including the Lord's Prayer.

Blessing or Dismissal, or both. The Peace may then be exchanged.

On feasts or other days of special significance, the Collect of the Day, or one proper to the season, may precede the Blessing or Dismissal. On other days, either of the following, or one of the Collects from Evening Prayer or from Compline, may be so used

Blessed are you, O Lord, the God of our fathers, creator of the changes of day and night, giving rest to the weary, renewing the strength of those who are spent, bestowing upon us occasions of song in the evening. As you have protected us in the day that is past, so be with us in the coming night; keep us from every sin, every evil, and every fear; for you are our light and salvation, and the strength of our life. To you be glory for endless ages. *Amen.*

Almighty, everlasting God, let our prayer in your sight be as incense, the lifting up of our hands as the evening sacrifice. Give us grace to behold you, present in your Word and Sacraments, and to recognize you in the lives of those around us. Stir up in us the flame of that love which burned in the heart of your Son as he bore his passion, and let it burn in us to eternal life and to the ages of ages. *Amen.*

A bishop or priest may use the following or some other blessing or grace

The Lord bless you and keep you. *Amen.*
The Lord make his face to shine upon you
    and be gracious to you. *Amen.*
The Lord lift up his countenance upon you
    and give you peace. *Amen.*

A deacon or lay person using the preceding blessing substitutes "us" for "you."

A Dismissal may be used (adding "Alleluia, alleluia" in Easter Season)

The People respond

Thanks be to God.

In Easter Season the People respond

Thanks be to God. Alleluia, alleluia.

Apostles' Creed
and
Lord's Prayer

The Apostles' Creed
and The Lord's Prayer

The Apostles' Creed

I believe in God, the Father almighty,
   creator of heaven and earth.
I believe in Jesus Christ, his only Son, our Lord.
   He was conceived by the power
             of the Holy Spirit
      and born of the Virgin Mary.
   He suffered under Pontius Pilate,
      was crucified, died, and was buried.
   He descended to the dead.
   On the third day he rose again.
   He ascended into heaven,
      and is seated at the right hand of the Father.
   He will come again to judge the living
             and the dead.

I believe in the Holy Spirit,
   the holy catholic Church,
   the communion of saints,
   the forgiveness of sins,
   the resurrection of the body,
   and the life everlasting. Amen.

The Lord's Prayer

Our Father, who art in heaven,
   hallowed be thy Name,
   thy kingdom come,
   thy will be done,
      on earth as it is in heaven.
Give us this day our daily bread.
And forgive us our trespasses,
   as we forgive those
      who trespass against us.
And lead us not into temptation,
   but deliver us from evil.
For thine is the kingdom,
   and the power, and the glory,
   for ever and ever. Amen.

or this

Our Father in heaven,
   hallowed be your Name,
   your kingdom come,
   your will be done,
     on earth as in heaven.
Give us today our daily bread.
Forgive us our sins
   as we forgive those
     who sin against us.
Save us from the time of trial,
   and deliver us from evil.
For the kingdom, the power,
   and the glory are yours,
     now and for ever. Amen.

Compline

An Order For Compline

The Officiant begins

The Lord Almighty grant us a peaceful night and a perfect end. *Amen.*

Officiant   Our help is in the Name of the Lord;
People   The maker of heaven and earth.

The Officiant may then say

Let us confess our sins to God.

Officiant and People

Almighty God, our heavenly Father:
We have sinned against you,
through our own fault,
in thought, and word, and deed,
and in what we have left undone.

For the sake of your Son our Lord Jesus Christ,
forgive us all our offenses;
and grant that we may serve you
in newness of life,
to the glory of your Name. Amen.

Officiant

May the Almighty God grant us forgiveness of
all our sins, and the grace and comfort of the
Holy Spirit. *Amen.*

The Officiant then says

       O God, make speed to save us.
People   O Lord, make haste to help us.

Officiant and People

Glory to the Father, and to the Son, and to the
Holy Spirit: as it was in the beginning, is now,
and will be for ever. Amen.

Except in Lent, add   Alleluia.

*One or more of the following Psalms are sung or said.
Other suitable selections may be substituted.*

Psalm 4   *Cum invocarem*

1 Answer me when I call, O God, defender
           of my cause; *
        you set me free when I am hard-pressed;
        have mercy on me and hear my prayer.

2 "You mortals, how long will you dishonor
           my glory? *
        how long will you worship dumb idols
        and run after false gods?"

3 Know that the LORD does wonders for
           the faithful; *
        when I call upon the LORD, he will hear me.

4 Tremble, then, and do not sin; *
        speak to your heart in silence upon your bed.

5 Offer the appointed sacrifices *
        and put your trust in the LORD.

6 Many are saying, "Oh, that we might see
           better times!" *
        Lift up the light of your countenance upon us,
           O LORD.

7   You have put gladness in my heart, *
        more than when grain and wine and oil increas

8   I lie down in peace; at once I fall asleep; *
        for only you, LORD, make me dwell in safety.

Psalm 31   *In te, Domine, speravi*

1   In you, O LORD, have I taken refuge;
    let me never be put to shame: *
        deliver me in your righteousness.

2   Incline your ear to me; *
        make haste to deliver me.

3   Be my strong rock, a castle to keep me safe,
    for you are my crag and my stronghold; *
        for the sake of your Name, lead me and
            guide me.

4   Take me out of the net that they have secretly
            set for me, *
        for you are my tower of strength.

5   Into your hands I commend my spirit, *
        for you have redeemed me,
        O LORD, O God of truth.

Psalm 91 *Qui habitat*

1 He who dwells in the shelter of the Most High *
   abides under the shadow of the Almighty.

2 He shall say to the LORD,
   "You are my refuge and my stronghold, *
      my God in whom I put my trust."

3 He shall deliver you from the snare of the hunter *
      and from the deadly pestilence.

4 He shall cover you with his pinions,
   and you shall find refuge under his wings; *
      his faithfulness shall be a shield and buckler.

5 You shall not be afraid of any terror by night, *
      nor of the arrow that flies by day;

6 Of the plague that stalks in the darkness, *
      nor of the sickness that lays waste at mid-day.

7 A thousand shall fall at your side
   and ten thousand at your right hand, *
      but it shall not come near you.

8 Your eyes only have to behold *
      to see the reward of the wicked.

9 Because you have made the LORD your refuge, *
   and the Most High your habitation,

10 There shall no evil happen to you, *
   neither shall any plague come near your
      dwelling.

11 For he shall give his angels charge over you, *
   to keep you in all your ways.

12 They shall bear you in their hands, *
   lest you dash your foot against a stone.

13 You shall tread upon the lion and adder; *
   you shall trample the young lion and the
      serpent under your feet.

14 Because he is bound to me in love,
   therefore will I deliver him; *
      I will protect him, because he knows my Name.

15 He shall call upon me, and I will answer him; *
   I am with him in trouble;
   I will rescue him and bring him to honor.

16 With long life will I satisfy him, *
   and show him my salvation.

Psalm 134 *Ecce nunc*

1 Behold now, bless the LORD, all you servants
     of the LORD, *
  you that stand by night in the house
     of the LORD.

2 Lift up your hands in the holy place and bless
     the LORD; *
  the LORD who made heaven and earth
     bless you out of Zion.

At the end of the Psalms is sung or said

Glory to the Father, and to the Son, and to the
  Holy Spirit: *
as it was in the beginning, is now, and will be
  for ever. Amen.

*One of the following, or some other suitable passage
of Scripture, is read*

Lord, you are in the midst of us, and we are
called by your Name: Do not forsake us, O
Lord our God.   *Jeremiah 14:9-22*

People   Thanks be to God.

or the following

Come to me, all who labor and are heavy-laden, and I will give you rest. Take my yoke upon you, and learn from me; for I am gentle and lowly in heart, and you will find rest for your souls. For my yoke is easy, and my burden is light.   *Matthew 11:28-30*

People   Thanks be to God.

or this

May the God of peace, who brought again from the dead our Lord Jesus, the great shepherd of the sheep, by the blood of the eternal convenant, equip you with everything good that you may do his will, working in you that which is pleasing in his sight, through Jesus Christ; to whom be glory for ever and ever.
Hebrews 13:20-21

People   Thanks be to God.

or this

Be sober, be watchful. Your adversary the devil prowls around like a roaring lion, seeking someone to devour. Resist him, firm in your faith.   *1 Peter 5:8-9a*

People   Thanks be to God.

A hymn suitable for the evening may be sung.

Then follows

V.   Into your hands, O Lord, I commend
          my spirit;
R.   For you have redeemed me, O Lord,
          O God of truth.
V.   Keep us, O Lord, as the apple of your eye;
R.   Hide us under the shadow of your wings.

Lord, have mercy.
Christ, have mercy.
Lord, have mercy.

*Officiant and People read one of these two versions
of the Lord's Prayer*

Our Father, who art in heaven,
   hallowed be thy Name,
   thy kingdom come,
   thy will be done,
      on earth as it is in heaven.

Give us this day our daily bread.
And forgive us our trespasses,
    as we forgive those
        who trespass against us.
And lead us not into temptation,
    but deliver us from evil.

or this

Our Father in heaven,
    hallowed be your Name,
    your kingdom come,
    your will be done,
        on earth as in heaven.
Give us today our daily bread.
Forgive us our sins
    as we forgive those
        who sin against us.
Save us from the time of trial,
    and deliver us from evil.

Officiant   Lord, hear our prayer;
People   And let our cry come to you.
Officiant   Let us pray.

The Officiant then says one of the following Collects

Be our light in the darkness, O Lord, and in your great mercy defend us from all perils and dangers of this night; for the love of your only Son, our Savior Jesus Christ. *Amen.*

Be present, O merciful God, and protect us through the hours of this night, so that we who are wearied by the changes and chances of this life may rest in your eternal changelessness; through Jesus Christ our Lord. *Amen.*

Look down, O Lord, from your heavenly throne, and illumine this night with your celestial brightness; that by night as by day your people may glorify your holy Name; through Jesus Christ our Lord. *Amen.*

Visit this place, O Lord, and drive far from it all snares of the enemy; let your holy angels dwell with us to preserve us in peace; and let your blessing be upon us always; through Jesus Christ our Lord. *Amen.*

A Collect for Saturdays

We give you thanks, O God, for revealing your
Son Jesus Christ to us by the light of his resurrection: Grant that as we sing your glory at the
close of this day, our joy may abound in the
morning as we celebrate the Paschal mystery;
through Jesus Christ our Lord. *Amen.*

One of the following prayers may be added

Keep watch, dear Lord, with those who work,
or watch, or weep this night, and give your angels charge over those who sleep. Tend the sick,
Lord Christ; give rest to the weary, bless the
dying, soothe the suffering, pity the afflicted,
shield the joyous; and all for your love's sake.
Amen.

or this

O God, your unfailing providence sustains the
world we live in and the life we live: Watch over
those, both night and day, who work while
others sleep, and grant that we may never forget

that our common life depends upon each other's toil; through Jesus Christ our Lord. *Amen.*

Silence may be kept, and free intercessions and thanksgivings may be offered.

The service concludes with the Song of Simeon with this Antiphon, which is sung or said by all

Guide us waking, O Lord, and guard us sleeping; that awake we may watch with Christ, and asleep we may rest in peace.

In Easter Season, add Alleluia, alleluia, alleluia.

Lord, you now have set your servant free *
    to go in peace as you have promised;

For these eyes of mine have seen the Savior, *
    whom you have prepared for all the world to see:

A Light to enlighten the nations, *
    and the glory of your people Israel.

Glory to the Father, and the Son, and to the
        Holy Spirit: *
    as it was in the beginning, is now, and will be
        for ever. Amen.

All repeat the Antiphon

Guide us waking, O Lord, and guard us sleeping; that awake we may watch with Christ, and asleep we may rest in peace.

In Easter Season, add   Alleluia, alleluia, alleluia.

Officiant Let us bless the Lord.
People   Thanks be to God.

The Officiant concludes

The almighty and merciful Lord, Father, Son, and Holy Spirit, bless us and keep us. *Amen.*

Reconciliation

Concerning the Rite

The ministry of reconciliation, which has been committed by Christ to his Church, is exercised through the care each Christian has for others, through the common prayer of Christians assembled for public worship, and through the priesthood of the Church and its ministers declaring absolution.

The Reconciliation of a Penitent is available for all who desire it. It is not restricted to times of sickness. Confessions may be heard anytime and anywhere.

Two equivalent forms of service are provided here to meet the needs of penitents. The absolution in these services may be pronounced only by a bishop or priest. Another Christian may be asked to hear a confession, but it must be made clear to the penitent that absolution will not be pronounced; instead, a declaration of forgiveness is provided.

When a confession is heard in a church building, the confessor may sit inside the altar rails or in a place set aside to give greater privacy, and the penitent kneels nearby. If preferred, the confessor and penitent may sit face to face for a spiritual conference leading to absolution or a declaration of forgiveness.

When the penitent has confessed all serious sins troubling the conscience and has given evidence of due contrition, the priest gives such counsel and encouragement as are needed and pronounces absolution. Before giving absolution, the priest may assign to the penitent a psalm, prayer, or hymn to be said, or something to be done, as a sign of penitence and act of thanksgiving.

The content of a confession is not normally a matter of subsequent discussion. The secrecy of a confession is morally absolute for the confessor, and must under no circumstances be broken.

Reconciliation 63

The Reconciliation
of a Penitent

Form One

The Penitent begins

Bless me, for I have sinned.

The Priest says

The Lord be in your heart and upon your lips that you may truly and humbly confess your sins: In the Name of the Father, and of the Son, and of the Holy Spirit. *Amen.*

Penitent

I confess to Almighty God, to his Church, and to you, that I have sinned by my own fault in thought, word, and deed, in things done and left undone; especially ＿＿＿＿＿ . For these and all other sins which I cannot now remember, I am truly sorry. I pray God to have mercy on me. I firmly intend amendment of life, and I humbly beg forgiveness of God and his Church, and ask you for counsel, direction, and absolution.

The Priest may offer counsel, direction, and comfort.

The Priest then pronounces this absolution

Our Lord Jesus Christ, who has left power to his Church to absolve all sinners who truly repent and believe in him, of his great mercy forgive you all your offenses; and by his authority committed to me, I absolve you from all your sins: In the Name of the Father, and of the Son, and of the Holy Spirit. *Amen.*

or this

Our Lord Jesus Christ, who offered himself to be sacrificed for us to the Father, and who conferred power on his Church to forgive sins, absolve you through my ministry by the grace of the Holy Spirit, and restore you in the perfect peace of the Church. *Amen.*

The Priest adds

The Lord has put away all your sins.

Penitent   Thanks be to God.

The Priest concludes

Go (or abide) in peace, and pray for me, a sinner.

Declaration of Forgiveness to be used by a Deacon or Lay Person

Our Lord Jesus Christ, who offered himself to be sacrificed for us to the Father, forgives your sins by the grace of the Holy Spirit. *Amen.*

Form Two

The Priest and Penitent begin as follows

Have mercy on me, O God, according to
        your loving-kindness;
    in your great compassion blot out my offenses.
Wash me through and through from my
        wickedness,
    and cleanse me from my sin.

For I know my transgressions only too well,
and my sin is ever before me.

Holy God, Holy and Mighty, Holy Immortal One,
have mercy upon us.

Penitent   Pray for me, a sinner.

Priest

May God in his love enlighten your heart, that
you may remember in truth all your sins and his
unfailing mercy. *Amen.*

*The Priest may then say one or more of these or
other appropriate verses of Scripture, first saying*

Hear the Word of God to all who truly turn to
him.

Come unto me, all ye that travail and are heavy
laden, and I will refresh you.   *Matthew 11:28*

God so loved the world, that he gave his only-
begotten Son, to the end that all that believe in
him should not perish, but have everlasting
life.   *John 3:16*

This is a true saying, and worthy of all men to be received, that Christ Jesus came into the world to save sinners.   *1 Timothy 1:15*

If any man sin, we have an Advocate with the Father, Jesus Christ the righteous; and he is the perfect offering for our sins, and not for ours only, but for the sins of the whole world.
1 John 2:1-2

The Priest then continues

Now, in the presence of Christ, and of me, his minister, confess your sins with a humble and obedient heart to Almighty God, our Creator and our Redeemer.

The Penitent says

Holy God, heavenly Father, you formed me from the dust in your image and likeness, and redeemed me from sin and death by the cross of your Son Jesus Christ. Through the water of baptism you clothed me with the shining garment of his righteousness, and established me among your children in your kingdom. But I have squandered the inheritance of your saints, and have wandered far in a land that is waste.

Especially, I confess to you and to the Church . . .

Here the penitent confesses particular sins.

Therefore, O Lord, from these and all other sins I cannot now remember, I turn to you in sorrow and repentance. Receive me again into the arms of your mercy, and restore me to the blessed company of your faithful people; through him in whom you have redeemed the world, your Son our Savior Jesus Christ. Amen.

The Priest may offer words of comfort and counsel.

Priest

Will you turn again to Christ as your Lord?

Penitent   I will.

Priest

Do you, then, forgive those who have sinned against you?

Penitent   I forgive them.

Priest

May Almighty God in mercy receive your confession of sorrow and of faith, strengthen you in all goodness, and by the power of the Holy Spirit keep you in eternal life. *Amen.*

*The Priest then lays a hand upon the penitent's head
(or extends a hand over the penitent),
saying one of the following*

Our Lord Jesus Christ, who offered himself to be sacrificed for us to the Father, and who conferred power on his Church to forgive sins, absolve you through my ministry by the grace of the Holy Spirit, and restore you in the perfect peace of the Church. *Amen.*

or this

Our Lord Jesus Christ, who has left power to his Church to absolve all sinners who truly repent and believe in him, of his great mercy forgive you all your offenses; and by his authority committed to me, I absolve you from all your sins: In the Name of the Father, and of the Son, and of the Holy Spirit. *Amen.*

The Priest concludes

Now there is rejoicing in heaven; for you were lost, and are found; you were dead, and are now alive in Christ Jesus our Lord. Go (*or* abide) in peace. The Lord has put away all your sins.

Penitent   Thanks be to God.

Declaration of Forgiveness
to be used by a Deacon or Lay Person

Our Lord Jesus Christ, who offered himself to be sacrificed for us to the Father, forgives your sins by the grace of the Holy Spirit. *Amen.*

Prayers

Index to Prayers

The Church

The Spiritual Life

The World

Prayers

For all Baptized Persons

Grant, Lord God, to all who have been baptized into the death and resurrection of your Son Jesus Christ, that, as we have put away the old life of sin, so we may be renewed in the spirit of our minds, and live in righteousness and true holiness; through Jesus Christ our Lord, who lives and reigns with you, in the unity of the Holy Spirit, one God, now and for ever. *Amen.*

For those about to be Baptized or to renew their Baptismal Commitment

O God, you prepared your disciples for the coming of the Spirit through the teaching of your Son Jesus Christ: Make the hearts and minds of your servants ready to receive the blessing of the Holy Spirit, that they may be filled with the strength of his presence; through Jesus Christ our Lord. *Amen.*

For a Birthday

O God, our times are in your hand: Look with favor, we pray, on your servant *N.* as *he* begins another year. Grant that *he* may grow in wisdom and grace, and strengthen *his* trust in your goodness all the days of *his* life; through Jesus Christ our Lord. *Amen.*

For a Church Convention or Meeting

Almighty and everliving God, source of all wisdom and understanding, be present with those who take counsel [in _____] for the renewal and mission of your Church. Teach us in all things to seek first your honor and glory. Guide us to perceive what is right, and grant us both the courage to pursue it and the grace to accomplish it; through Jesus Christ our Lord. *Amen.*

For Clergy and People

Almighty and everlasting God, from whom cometh every good and perfect gift: Send down upon our bishops, and other clergy, and upon the congregations committed to their charge, the healthful Spirit of thy grace; and, that they may truly please thee, pour upon them the continual dew of thy blessing. Grant this, O Lord, for the honor of our Advocate and Mediator, Jesus Christ. *Amen.*

For the Conservation of Natural Resources

Heavenly Father, generous Provider of all good gifts, teach us to live wisely on this fair earth. Bless our efforts to restore a healthful environment, to make the air clean, the water pure, and the soil rich. Let food abound on land and sea, and grant that it may be so distributed that hunger may threaten the world no more; through Jesus Christ our Lord. *Amen.*

For the Departed

O God, whose mercies cannot be numbered: Accept our prayers on behalf of your servant N., and grant *him* an entrance into the land of light and joy, in the fellowship of your saints; through Jesus Christ our Lord, who lives and reigns with you and the Holy Spirit, one God, now and for ever. *Amen.*

Father of all, we pray to you for N., and for all those whom we love but see no longer. Grant to them eternal rest. Let light perpetual shine upon them. May *his* soul and the souls of all the departed, through the mercy of God, rest in peace. *Amen.*

For the Diocese

O God, by your Grace you have called us in this Diocese to a goodly fellowship of faith. Bless our Bishop(s) N. [and N.], and other clergy, and all our people. Grant that your Word may be truly preached and truly heard, your Sacraments faithfully administered and faithfully received. By your Spirit, fashion our lives according to the example of your Son, and grant that we may show the power of your love to all among whom we live; through Jesus Christ our Lord. *Amen.*

For Guidance

Heavenly Father, in you we live and move and have our being: We humbly pray you so to guide and govern us by your Holy Spirit, that in all the cares and occupations of our life we may not forget you, but may remember that we are ever walking in your sight; through Jesus Christ our Lord. *Amen.*

O God of peace, *who hast* taught us that in returning and rest we shall be saved, in quietness and in confidence shall be our strength: By the might of *thy* Spirit lift us, we pray *thee,* to *thy* presence, where we may be still and know that *thou art* God; through Jesus Christ our Lord. *Amen.*

Of the Holy Spirit

Almighty and most merciful God, grant that by the indwelling of your Holy Spirit we may be enlightened and strengthened for your service; through Jesus Christ our Lord, who lives and reigns with you, in the unity of the Holy Spirit, one God, now and for ever. *Amen.*

Of the Incarnation

O God, who wonderfully created, and yet more wonderfully restored, the dignity of human nature: Grant that we may share the divine life of him who humbled himself to share our humanity, your Son Jesus Christ; who lives and reigns with you, in the unity of the Holy Spirit, one God, for ever and ever. *Amen.*

For Joy in God's Creation

O heavenly Father, *who hast* filled the world with beauty: Open our eyes to behold *thy* gracious hand in all *thy* works; that, rejoicing in *thy* whole creation, we may learn to serve *thee* with gladness; for the sake of him through whom all things were made, *thy* Son Jesus Christ our Lord. *Amen.*

We give you thanks, most gracious God, for the beauty of earth and sky and sea; for the richness of mountains, plains, and rivers; for the songs of birds and the loveliness of flowers. We praise you for these good gifts, and pray that we may safeguard them for our prosperity. Grant that we may continue to grow in our grateful enjoyment of your abundant creation, to the honor and glory of your Name, now and for ever. *Amen.*

For Married Couples

Almighty God, giver of life and love, bless *N.* and *N.* Grant them wisdom and devotion in the ordering of their common life, that each may be to the other a strength in need, a counselor in perplexity, a comfort in sorrow, and a companion in joy. And so knit their wills together in

your will and their spirits in your Spirit, that
they may live together in love and peace all the
days of their life; through Jesus Christ our
Lord. *Amen.*

For the Mission of the Church

Almighty and everlasting God, by whose Spirit
the whole body of your faithful people is gov-
erned and sanctified: Receive our supplications
and prayers which we offer before you for all
members of your holy Church, that in their vo-
cation and ministry they may truly and de-
voutly serve you; through our Lord and Savior
Jesus Christ. *Amen.*

Lord Jesus Christ, you stretched out your arms
of love on the hard wood of the cross that everyone might come within the reach of your
saving embrace: So clothe us in your Spirit that
we, reaching forth our hands in love, may bring
those who do not know you to the knowledge
and love of you; for the honor of your Name.
Amen.

For Monastic Orders and Vocations

O Lord Jesus Christ, you became poor for our sake, that we might be made rich through your poverty: Guide and sanctify, we pray, those whom you call to follow you under the vows of poverty, chastity, and obedience, that by their prayer and service they may enrich your Church, and by their life and worship may glorify your Name; for you reign with the Father and the Holy Spirit, one God, now and for ever. *Amen.*

For the Nation

Lord God Almighty, you have made all the peoples of the earth for your glory, to serve you in freedom and in peace: Give to the people of our country a zeal for justice and the strength of forbearance, that we may use our liberty in accordance with your gracious will; through Jesus Christ our Lord, who lives and reigns with you and the Holy Spirit, one God, for ever and ever. *Amen.*

Almighty God, who hast given us this good land for our heritage: We humbly beseech thee that we may always prove ourselves a people mindful of thy favor and glad to do thy will. Bless our land with honorable industry, sound learning, and pure manners. Save us from violence, discord, and confusion; from pride and arrogance, and from every evil way. Defend our liberties, and fashion into one united people the multitudes brought hither out of many kindreds and tongues. Endue with the spirit of wisdom those to whom in thy Name we entrust the authority of government, that there may be justice and peace at home, and that, through obedience to thy law, we may show forth thy praise among the nations of the earth. In the time of prosperity, fill our hearts with thankfulness, and in the day of trouble, suffer not our trust in thee to fail; all which we ask through Jesus Christ our Lord. *Amen.*

For the Parish

Almighty and everliving God, ruler of all things in heaven and earth, hear our prayers for this parish family. Strengthen the faithful, arouse the careless, and restore the penitent. Grant us all things necessary for our common life, and bring us all to be of one heart and mind within your holy Church; through Jesus Christ our Lord. *Amen.*

For Peace

Most holy God, the source of all good desires, all right judgments, and all just works: Give to us, your servants, that peace which the world cannot give, so that our minds may be fixed on the doing of your will, and that we, being delivered from the fear of all enemies, may live in peace and quietness; through the mercies of Christ Jesus our Savior. *Amen.*

Almighty God, kindle, we pray, in every heart the true love of peace, and guide with your wisdom those who take counsel for the nations of the earth, that in tranquillity your dominion may increase until the earth is filled with the knowledge of your love; through Jesus Christ our Lord, who lives and reigns with you, in the unity of the Holy Spirit, one God, now and for ever. *Amen.*

For a Person in Trouble or Bereavement

O merciful Father, who hast taught us in thy holy Word that thou dost not willingly afflict or grieve the children of men: Look with pity upon the sorrows of thy servant for whom our prayers are offered. Remember *him,* O Lord, in mercy, nourish *his* soul with patience, comfort *him* with a sense of thy goodness, lift up thy countenance upon *him,* and give *him* peace; through Jesus Christ our Lord. *Amen.*

Of the Resurrection

Almighty and everlasting God, who in the Paschal mystery established the new covenant of reconciliation: Grant that all who have been reborn into the fellowship of Christ's Body may show forth in their lives what they profess by their faith; through Jesus Christ our Lord, who lives and reigns with you and the Holy Spirit, one God, for ever and ever. *Amen.*

For a Retreat

O Lord Jesus Christ, who went apart to pray with your disciples: Grant to your servants in *this* retreat (*or,* in the retreat for . . . in . . .) that *we* may rest a while with you and know that you have found us long before. Let the words that shall be spoken here not fall on barren ground, but, enriched by prayer and silence, bear good fruit in our lives to the glory of your holy Name. *Amen.*

A Prayer attributed to St. Francis

Lord, make us instruments of your peace. Where there is hatred, let us sow love; where there is injury, pardon; where there is discord, union; where there is doubt, faith; where there is despair, hope; where there is darkness, light; where there is sadness, joy. Grant that we may not so much seek to be consoled as to console; to be understood as to understand; to be loved as to love. For it is in giving that we receive; it is in pardoning that we are pardoned; and it is in dying that we are born to eternal life. *Amen.*

For Schools and Colleges

O Eternal God, bless all schools, colleges, and universities [and especially _____], that they may be lively centers for sound learning, new discovery, and the pursuit of wisdom; and grant that those who teach and those who learn may find you to be the source of all truth; through Jesus Christ our Lord. *Amen.*

For Self-Acceptance

God, give us the serenity to accept the things we cannot change, the courage to change the things we can, and the wisdom to distinguish the one from the other. *Amen.*

For Self-Dedication

Make us channels of your grace, O Lord, that our wills may conform to your will and our choices reflect your love to your people; so that your law may be fulfilled on earth as it is in heaven; through Jesus Christ our Lord. *Amen.*

For Recovery from Sickness

O God, the strength of the weak and the comfort of sufferers: Mercifully accept our prayers, and grant to your servant N. the help of your power, that *his* sickness may be turned into health, and our sorrow into joy; through Jesus Christ our Lord. *Amen.*

For the Sanctification of Illness

Sanctify, O Lord, the sickness of your servant N., that the sense of *his* weakness may add strength to *his* faith and seriousness to *his* repentance; and grant that *he* may live with you in everlasting life; through Jesus Christ our Lord. *Amen.*

For Thanksgiving

Accept, O Lord, our thanks and praise for all that you have done for us. We thank you for the splendor of the whole creation, for the beauty of this world, for the wonder of life, and for the mystery of love.

We thank you for the blessing of family and friends, and for the loving care which surrounds us on every side.

We thank you for setting us at tasks which demand our best efforts, and for leading us to accomplishments which satisfy and delight us.

We thank you also for those disappointments and failures that lead us to acknowledge our dependence on you alone.

Above all, we thank you for your Son Jesus Christ; for the truth of his Word and the example of his life; for his steadfast obedience, by which he overcame temptation; for his dying, through which he overcame death; and for his rising to life again, in which we are raised to the life of your kingdom.

Grant us the gift of your Spirit, that we may know him and make him known; and through him, at all times and in all places, may give thanks to you in all things. *Amen.*

For those we Love

Almighty God, we entrust all who are dear to us to *thy* never-failing care and love, for this life and the life to come, knowing that *thou art* doing for them better things than we can desire or pray for; through Jesus Christ our Lord. *Amen.*

For Travelers

O God, our heavenly Father, whose glory fills the whole creation, and whose presence we find wherever we go: Preserve those who travel [in particular _____]; surround them with your loving care; protect them from every danger; and bring them in safety to their journey's end; through Jesus Christ our Lord. *Amen.*

For the Unity of the Church

Almighty Father, whose blessed Son before his passion prayed for his disciples that they might be one, as you and he are one: Grant that your Church, being bound together in love and obedience to you, may be united in one body by the one Spirit, that the world may believe in him whom you have sent, your Son Jesus Christ our Lord; who lives and reigns with you, in the unity of the Holy Spirit, one God, now and for ever. *Amen.*

Before Receiving Communion

Almighty Father, whose dear Son, on the night before he suffered, instituted the Sacrament of his Body and Blood: Mercifully grant that we may receive it thankfully in remembrance of Jesus Christ our Lord, who in these holy mysteries gives us a pledge of eternal life; and who now lives and reigns with you and the Holy Spirit, one God, for ever and ever. *Amen.*

Be present, be present, O Jesus, our great High Priest, as you were present with your disciples, and be known to us in the breaking of bread; who lives and reigns with the Father and the Holy Spirit, now and for ever. *Amen.*

After Receiving Communion

God our Father, whose Son our Lord Jesus Christ in a wonderful Sacrament has left us a memorial of his passion: Grant us so to venerate the sacred mysteries of his Body and Blood, that we may ever perceive within ourselves the fruit of his redemption; who lives and reigns with you and the Holy Spirit, one God, for ever and ever. *Amen.*

Almighty and everliving God, we thank you for feeding us with the spiritual food of the most precious Body and Blood of your Son our Savior Jesus Christ; and for assuring us in these holy mysteries that we are living members of the Body of your Son, and heirs of your eternal kingdom. And now, Father, send us out to do the work you have given us to do, to love and serve you as faithful witnesses of Christ our Lord. To him, to you, and to the Holy Spirit, be honor and glory, now and for ever. *Amen.*

Eternal God, heavenly Father, you have graciously accepted us as living members of your Son our Savior Jesus Christ, and you have fed us with spiritual food in the Sacrament of his Body and Blood. Send us now into the world in peace, and grant us strength and courage to love and serve you with gladness and singleness of heart; through Christ our Lord. *Amen.*

Prayers for Use by a Sick Person

For Trust in God

O God, the source of all health: So fill my heart with faith in your love, that with calm expectancy I may make room for your power to possess me, and gracefully accept your healing; through Jesus Christ our Lord. Amen.

In Pain

Lord Jesus Christ, by your patience in suffering you hallowed earthly pain and gave us the example of obedience to your Father's will: Be near me in my time of weakness and pain; sustain me by your grace, that my strength and courage may not fail; heal me according to your will; and help me always to believe that what happens to me here is of little account if you hold me in eternal life, my Lord and my God. Amen.

For Sleep

O heavenly Father, you give your children sleep for the refreshing of soul and body: Grant me this gift, I pray; keep me in that perfect peace which you have promised to those whose minds are fixed on you; and give me such a sense of your presence, that in the hours of silence I may enjoy the blessed assurance of your love; through Jesus Christ our Savior. Amen.

In the Morning

This is another day, O Lord. I know not what it will bring forth, but make me ready, Lord, for whatever it may be. If I am to stand up, help me to stand bravely. If I am to sit still, help me to sit quietly. If I am to lie low, help me to do it patiently. And if I am to do nothing, let me do it gallantly. Make these words more than words, and give me the Spirit of Jesus. Amen.

Seasonal Prayers

First Sunday of Advent

Almighty God, give us grace to cast away the works of darkness, and put on the armor of light, now in the time of this mortal life in which your son Jesus Christ came to visit us in great humility; that in the last day, when he shall come again in his glorious majesty to judge both the living and the dead, we may rise to the life immortal; through him who lives and reigns with you and the Holy Spirit, one God, now and for ever. *Amen.*

The Nativity of Our Lord: Christmas Day   *December 25*

O God, you make us glad by the yearly festival of the birth of your only Son Jesus Christ: Grant that we, who joyfully receive him as our Redeemer, may with sure confidence behold him when he comes to be our Judge; who lives and reigns with you and the Holy Spirit, one God, now and for ever. *Amen.*

First Sunday after Christmas Day

Almighty God, you have poured upon us the new light of your incarnate Word: Grant that this light, enkindled in our hearts, may shine forth in our lives; through Jesus Christ our Lord, who lives and reigns with you, in the unity of the Holy Spirit, one God, now and for ever. *Amen.*

The Epiphany *January 6*

O God, by the leading of a star you manifested your only Son to the peoples of the earth: Lead us, who know you now by faith, to your presence, where we may see your glory face to face; through Jesus Christ our Lord, who lives and reigns with you and the Holy Spirit, one God, now and for ever. *Amen.*

Ash Wednesday

Almighty and everlasting God, you hate nothing you have made and forgive the sins of all who are penitent: Create and make in us new and contrite hearts, that we, worthily lamenting our sins and acknowledging our wretchedness, may obtain of you, the God of all mercy, perfect remission and forgiveness; through Jesus Christ our Lord, who lives and reigns with you and the Holy Spirit, one God, for ever and ever. *Amen.*

Holy Week

Almighty God, whose most dear Son went not up to joy but first he suffered pain, and entered not into glory before he was crucified: Mercifully grant that we, walking in the way of the cross, may find it none other than the way of life and peace; through Jesus Christ your Son our Lord, who lives and reigns with you and the Holy Spirit, one God, for ever and ever. *Amen.*

Good Friday

Almighty God, we pray you graciously to behold this your family, for whom our Lord Jesus Christ was willing to be betrayed, and given into the hands of sinners, and to suffer death upon the cross; who now lives and reigns with you and the Holy Spirit, one God, for ever and ever. *Amen.*

Easter Day

Almighty God, who through your only-begotten Son Jesus Christ overcame death and opened to us the gate of everlasting life: Grant that we, who celebrate with joy the day of the Lord's resurrection, may be raised from the death of sin by your life-giving Spirit; through Jesus Christ our Lord, who lives and reigns with you and the Holy Spirit, one God, now and for ever. *Amen.*

Ascension Day

Grant, we pray, Almighty God, that as we believe your only-begotten Son our Lord Jesus Christ to have ascended into heaven, so we may also in heart and mind there ascend, and with him continually dwell; who lives and reigns with you and the Holy Spirit, one God, for ever and ever. *Amen.*

The Day of Pentecost: Whitsunday

O God, who on this day taught the hearts of your faithful people by sending to them the light of your Holy Spirit: Grant us by the same Spirit to have a right judgment in all things, and evermore to rejoice in his holy comfort;

through Jesus Christ your Son our Lord, who lives and reigns with you, in the unity of the Holy Spirit, one God, for ever and ever. *Amen.*

All Saints' Day   November 1

Almighty God, you have knit together your elect in one communion and fellowship in the mystical body of your Son Christ our Lord: Give us grace so to follow your blessed saints in all virtuous and godly living, that we may come to those ineffable joys that you have prepared for those who truly love you; through Jesus Christ our Lord, who with you and the Holy Spirit lives and reigns, one God, in glory everlasting. *Amen.*

Psalms
and Canticles

Table of Psalms

Psalms and Canticles

15 *Domine, quis habitabit?*

1 LORD, who may dwell in your tabernacle? *
    who may abide upon your holy hill?

2 Whoever leads a blameless life and does
        what is right, *
    who speaks the truth from his heart.

3 There is no guile upon his tongue;
    he does no evil to his friend; *
        he does not heap contempt upon his neighbor.

4 In his sight the wicked is rejected, *
    but he honors those who fear the LORD.

5 He has sworn to do no wrong *
    and does not take back his word.

6   He does not give his money in hope of gain, *
        nor does he take a bribe against the innocent.

7   Whoever does these things *
        shall never be overthrown.

22   *Deus, Deus meus*

1   My God, my God, why have you forsaken me? *
        and are so far from my cry
        and from the words of my distress?

2   O my God, I cry in the daytime, but you
            do not answer; *
        by night as well, but I find no rest.

3   Yet you are the Holy One, *
        enthroned upon the praises of Israel.

4   Our forefathers put their trust in you; *
        they trusted, and you delivered them.

5   They cried out to you and were delivered; *
        they trusted in you and were not put to shame.

6   But as for me, I am a worm and no man, *
        scorned by all and despised by the people.

7   All who see me laugh me to scorn; *
        they curl their lips and wag their heads, saying,

8   "He trusted in the Lord; let him deliver him; *
        let him rescue him, if he delights in him."

9   Yet you are he who took me out of the womb, *
        and kept me safe upon my mother's breast.

10   I have been entrusted to you ever since
            I was born; *
        you were my God when I was still in my
            mother's womb.

11   Be not far from me, for trouble is near, *
        and there is none to help.

23   *Dominus regit me*

1   The LORD is my shepherd; *
        I shall not be in want.

2   He makes me lie down in green pastures *
        and leads me beside still waters.

3   He revives my soul *
        and guides me along right pathways
            for his Name's sake.

4   Though I walk through the valley of the shadow
          of death,
    I shall fear no evil; *
       for you are with me;
       your rod and your staff, they comfort me.

5   You spread a table before me in the presence of
          those who trouble me; *
       you have anointed my head with oil,
       and my cup is running over.

6   Surely your goodness and mercy shall follow me
          all the days of my life, *
       and I will dwell in the house of the LORD
          for ever.

42   *Quemadmodum*

1   As the deer longs for the water-brooks, *
       so longs my soul for you, O God.

2   My soul is athirst for God, athirst
          for the living God; *
       when shall I come to appear before
          the presence of God?

3   My tears have been my food day and night, *
        while all day long they say to me,
      "Where now is your God?"

4   I pour out my soul when I think on these things: *
        how I went with the multitude and led them
            into the house of God,

5   With the voice of praise and thanksgiving, *
        among those who keep holy-day.

6   Why are you so full of heaviness, O my soul? *
        and why are you so disquieted within me?

7   Put your trust in God; *
        for I will yet give thanks to him,
        who is the help of my countenance, and my God

43   *Judica me, Deus*

1   Give judgment for me, O God,
        and defend my cause against an ungodly people; *
        deliver me from the deceitful and the wicked.

2   For you are the God of my strength;
        why have you put me from you? *

and why do I go so heavily while the enemy
   oppresses me?

3 Send out your light and your truth, that they
      may lead me, *
   and bring me to your holy hill
   and to your dwelling;

4 That I may go to the altar of God,
   to the God of my joy and gladness; *
      and on the harp I will give thanks to you,
         O God my God.

5 Why are you so full of heaviness, O my soul? *
   and why are you so disquieted within me?

6 Put your trust in God; *
      for I will yet give thanks to him,
      who is the help of my countenance, and my God.

46 *Deus noster refugium*

1 God is our refuge and strength, *
   a very present help in trouble.

2 Therefore we will not fear, though the earth
      be moved, *

and though the mountains be toppled into the
    depths of the sea;

3   Though its waters rage and foam, *
      and though the mountains tremble at its tumult.

4   The LORD of hosts is with us; *
      the God of Jacob is our stronghold.

5   There is a river whose streams make glad
        the city of God, *
      the holy habitation of the Most High.

6   God is in the midst of her;
    she shall not be overthrown; *
      God shall help her at the break of day.

7   The nations make much ado, and the kingdoms
        are shaken; *
      God has spoken, and the earth shall melt away.

8   The LORD of hosts is with us; *
      the God of Jacob is our stronghold.

9   Come now and look upon the works of the LORD,
      what awesome things he has done on earth.

10   It is he who makes war to cease in all the world; *
          he breaks the bow, and shatters the spear,
          and burns the shields with fire.

11   "Be still, then, and know that I am God; *
          I will be exalted among the nations;
          I will be exalted in the earth."

12   The LORD of hosts is with us; *
          the God of Jacob is our stronghold.

47   *Omnes gentes, plaudite*

1   Clap your hands, all you peoples; *
          shout to God with a cry of joy.

2   For the LORD Most High is to be feared; *
          he is the great King over all the earth.

3   He subdues the peoples under us, *
          and the nations under our feet.

4   He chooses our inheritance for us, *
          the pride of Jacob whom he loves.

5   God has gone up with a shout, *
          the LORD with the sound of the ram's-horn.

6   Sing praises to God, sing praises; *
      sing praises to our King, sing praises.

7   For God is King of all the earth; *
      sing praises with all your skill.

8   God reigns over the nations; *
      God sits upon his holy throne.

9   The nobles of the peoples have gathered together *
      with the people of the God of Abraham.

10 The rulers of the earth belong to God, *
      and he is highly exalted.

51   *Miserere mei, Deus*

1   Have mercy on me, O God, according to your
         loving-kindness; *
      in your great compassion blot out my offenses.

2   Wash me through and through from my
         wickedness *
      and cleanse me from my sin.

3   For I know my transgressions, *
      and my sin is ever before me.

4   Against you only have I sinned *
        and done what is evil in your sight.

5   And so you are justified when you speak *
        and upright in your judgment.

6   Indeed, I have been wicked from my birth, *
        a sinner from my mother's womb.

7   For behold, you look for truth deep within me, *
        and will make me understand wisdom secretly.

8   Purge me from my sin, and I shall be pure; *
        wash me, and I shall be clean indeed.

9   Make me hear of joy and gladness, *
        that the body you have broken may rejoice.

10 Hide your face from my sins *
        and blot out all my iniquities.

11 Create in me a clean heart, O God, *
        and renew a right spirit within me.

12 Cast me not away from your presence *
        and take not your holy Spirit from me.

13 Give me the joy of your saving help again *
        and sustain me with your bountiful Spirit.

Psalms   115

14   I shall teach your ways to the wicked, *
       and sinners shall return to you.

15   Deliver me from death, O God, *
       and my tongue shall sing of your righteousness,
         O God of my salvation.

16   Open my lips, O LORD, *
       and my mouth shall proclaim your praise.

17   Had you desired it, I would have
         offered sacrifice, *
       but you take no delight in burnt-offerings.

18   The sacrifice of God is a troubled spirit; *
       a broken and contrite heart, O God,
         you will not despise.

19   Be favorable and gracious to Zion, *
       and rebuild the walls of Jerusalem.

20   Then you will be pleased with the appointed
         sacrifices,
       with burnt-offerings and oblations; *
         then shall they offer young bullocks upon
           your altar.

67 *Deus misereatur*

1   May God be merciful to us and bless us, *
    show us the light of his countenance and
      come to us.

2   Let your ways be known upon earth, *
    your saving health among all nations.

3   Let the peoples praise you, O God; *
    let all the peoples praise you.

4   Let the nations be glad and sing for joy, *
    for you judge the peoples with equity
    and guide all the nations upon earth.

5   Let the peoples praise you, O God; *
    let all the peoples praise you.

6   The earth has brought forth her increase; *
    may God, our own God, give us his blessing.

7   May God give us his blessing, *
    and may all the ends of the earth stand
      in awe of him.

84 *Quam dilecta!*

1   How dear to me is your dwelling,
      O LORD of hosts! *
    My soul has a desire and longing for the courts
      of the LORD;
    my heart and my flesh rejoice in the living God.

2   The sparrow has found her a house
  and the swallow a nest where she may lay
      her young; *
    by the side of your altars, O LORD of hosts,
    my King and my God.

3   Happy are they who dwell in your house! *
    they will always be praising you.

4   Happy are the people whose strength is in you! *
    whose hearts are set on the pilgrims' way.

5   Those who go through the desolate valley will find
      it a place of springs, *
    for the early rains have covered it with pools
      of water.

6   They will climb from height to height, *
    and the God of gods will reveal himself in Zion.

7   LORD God of hosts, hear my prayer; *
        hearken, O God of Jacob.

8   Behold our defender, O God; *
        and look upon the face of your Anointed.

9   For one day in your courts is better than
            a thousand in my own room, *
        and to stand at the threshold of the house
            of my God
        than to dwell in the tents of the wicked.

10 For the LORD God is both sun and shield; *
        he will give grace and glory;

11 No good thing will the LORD withhold *
        from those who walk with integrity.

12 O LORD of hosts, *
        happy are they who put their trust in you!

95 *Venite, exultemus*

1   Come, let us sing to the LORD; *
        let us shout for joy to the Rock of our salvation.

2   Let us come before his presence with thanksgiving *
        and raise a loud shout to him with psalms.

3   For the LORD is a great God, *
        and a great King above all gods.

4   In his hand are the caverns of the earth, *
        and the heights of the hills are his also.

5   The sea is his, for he made it, *
        and his hands have molded the dry land.

6   Come, let us bow down, and bend the knee, *
        and kneel before the LORD our Maker.

7   For he is our God,
    and we are the people of his pasture and the
            sheep of his hand. *
        Oh, that today you would hearken to his voice!

IOO   *Jubilate Deo*

1   Be joyful in the LORD, all you lands; *
        serve the LORD with gladness
        and come before his presence with a song.

2   Know this: The LORD himself is God; *
        he himself has made us, and we are his;
        we are his people and the sheep of his pasture.

3   Enter his gates with thanksgiving;
    go into his courts with praise; *
        give thanks to him and call upon his Name.

4   For the LORD is good;
    his mercy is everlasting; *
        and his faithfulness endures from age to age.

103   *Benedic, anima mea*

1   Bless the LORD, O my soul, *
        and all that is within me, bless his holy Name.

2   Bless the LORD, O my soul, *
        and forget not all his benefits.

3   He forgives all your sins *
        and heals all your infirmities;

4   He redeems your life from the grave *
        and crowns you with mercy
            and loving-kindness;

5   He satisfies you with good things, *
        and your youth is renewed like an eagle's.

6   The LORD executes righteousness *
        and judgment for all who are oppressed.

7   He made his ways known to Moses *
        and his works to the children of Israel.

8   The LORD is full of compassion and mercy, *
        slow to anger and of great kindness.

9   He will not always accuse us, *
        nor will he keep his anger for ever.

10 He has not dealt with us according to our sins, *
        nor rewarded us according to our wickedness.

11 For as the heavens are high above the earth, *
        so is his mercy great upon those who fear him.

12 As far as the east is from the west, *
        so far has he removed our sins from us.

13 As a father cares for his children, *
        so does the LORD care for those who fear him.

14 For he himself knows whereof we are made; *
        he remembers that we are but dust.

15 Our days are like the grass; *
        we flourish like a flower of the field;

16 When the wind goes over it, it is gone, *
    and its place shall know it no more.

17 But the merciful goodness of the LORD endures
        for ever on those who fear him, *
    and his righteousness on children's children;

18 On those who keep his covenant *
    and remember his commandments and do them.

19 The LORD has set his throne in heaven, *
    and his kingship has dominion over all.

20 Bless the LORD, you angels of his,
    you mighty ones who do his bidding, *
    and hearken to the voice of his word.

21 Bless the LORD, all you his hosts, *
    you ministers of his who do his will.

22 Bless the LORD, all you works of his,
    in all places of his dominion; *
    bless the LORD, O my soul.

116 *Dilexi, quoniam*

1 I love the LORD, because he has heard the voice of
        my supplication, *

because he has inclined his ear to me whenever
    I called upon him.

10   How shall I repay the LORD *
        for all the good things he has done for me?

11   I will lift up the cup of salvation *
        and call upon the Name of the LORD.

12   I will fulfill my vows to the LORD *
        in the presence of all his people.

13   Precious in the sight of the LORD *
        is the death of his servants.

14   O LORD, I am your servant; *
        I am your servant and the child of
           your handmaid;
        you have freed me from my bonds.

15   I will offer you the sacrifice of thanksgiving *
        and call upon the Name of the LORD.

16   I will fulfill my vows to the LORD *
        in the presence of all his people,

17   In the courts of the LORD'S house, *
        in the midst of you, O Jerusalem.
        Hallelujah!

120 *Ad Dominum*

1 When I was in trouble, I called to the LORD; *
  I called to the LORD, and he answered me.

2 Deliver me, O LORD, from lying lips *
  and from the deceitful tongue.

3 What shall be done to you, and what more
          besides, *
  O you deceitful tongue?

4 The sharpened arrows of a warrior, *
  along with hot glowing coals.

5 How hateful it is that I must lodge in Meshech *
  and dwell among the tents of Kedar!

6 Too long have I had to live *
  among the enemies of peace.

7 I am on the side of peace, *
  but when I speak of it, they are for war.

122 *Lætatus sum*

1 I was glad when they said to me, *
  "Let us go to the house of the LORD."

2   Now our feet are standing *
        within your gates, O Jerusalem.

3   Jerusalem is built as a city *
        that is at unity with itself;

4   To which the tribes go up,
    the tribes of the LORD, *
        the assembly of Israel,
            to praise the Name of the LORD.

5   For there are the thrones of judgment, *
        the thrones of the house of David.

6   Pray for the peace of Jerusalem: *
        "May they prosper who love you.

7   Peace be within your walls *
        and quietness within your towers.

8   For my brethren and companions' sake, *
        I pray for your prosperity.

9   Because of the house of the LORD our God, *
        I will seek to do you good."

123 *Ad te levavi oculos meos*

1 To you I lift up my eyes, *
    to you enthroned in the heavens.

2 As the eyes of servants look to the hand of
        their masters, *
    and the eyes of a maid to the hand of
        her mistress,

3 So our eyes look to the LORD our God, *
    until he shows us his mercy.

4 Have mercy upon us, O LORD, have mercy, *
    for we have had more than enough of contempt,

5 Too much of the scorn of the indolent rich, *
    and of the derision of the proud.

124 *Nisi quia Dominus*

1 If the LORD had not been on our side, *
    let Israel now say;

2 If the LORD had not been on our side, *
    when enemies rose up against us;

3   Then would they have swallowed us up alive *
        in their fierce anger toward us;

4   Then would the waters have overwhelmed us *
        and the torrent gone over us;

5   Then would the raging waters *
        have gone right over us.

6   Blessed be the LORD! *
        he has not given us over to be a prey
            for their teeth.

7   We have escaped like a bird from the snare of
            the fowler; *
        the snare is broken, and we have escaped.

8   Our help is in the Name of the LORD, *
        the maker of heaven and earth.

125   *Qui confidunt*

1   Those who trust in the LORD are like Mount Zion,
        which cannot be moved, but stands fast for ever.

2   The hills stand about Jerusalem; *
        so does the LORD stand round about his people,

from this time forth for evermore.

3 The scepter of the wicked shall not hold sway
        over the land alloted to the just, *
    so that the just shall not put their hands to evil.

4 Show your goodness, O LORD, to those who
        are good *
    and to those who are true of heart.

5 As for those who turn aside to crooked ways,
    the LORD will lead them away with the evildoers; *
        but peace be upon Israel.

127 *Nisi Dominus*

1 Unless the LORD builds the house, *
    their labor is in vain who build it.

2 Unless the LORD watches over the city, *
    in vain the watchman keeps his vigil.

3 It is in vain that you rise so early and go to bed
        so late; *
    vain, too, to eat the bread of toil,
    for he gives to his beloved sleep.

4   Children are a heritage from the LORD, *
        and the fruit of the womb is a gift.

5   Like arrows in the hand of a warrior *
        are the children of one's youth.

6   Happy is the man who has his quiver full
            of them! *
        he shall not be put to shame
        when he contends with his enemies in the gate.

128   *Beati omnes*

1   Happy are they all who fear the LORD, *
        and who follow in his ways!

2   You shall eat the fruit of your labor; *
        happiness and prosperity shall be yours.

3   Your wife shall be like a fruitful vine within
            your house, *
        your children like olive shoots round about
            your table.

4   The man who fears the LORD *
        shall thus indeed be blessed.

5   The LORD bless you from Zion, *
        and may you see the prosperity of Jerusalem
            all the days of your life.

6   May you live to see your children's children; *
        may peace be upon Israel.

130   *De profundis*

1   Out of the depths have I called to you, O LORD;
    LORD, hear my voice; *
        let your ears consider well the voice of
            my supplication.

2   If you, LORD, were to note what is done amiss, *
        O LORD, who could stand?

3   For there is forgiveness with you; *
        therefore you shall be feared.

4   I wait for the LORD; my soul waits for him; *
        in his word is my hope.

5   My soul waits for the LORD,
    more than watchmen for the morning, *
        more than watchmen for the morning.

6 O Israel, wait for the LORD, *
      for with the LORD there is mercy;

7 With him there is plenteous redemption, *
      and he shall redeem Israel from all their sins.

133 *Ecce, quam bonum!*

1 Oh, how good and pleasant it is, *
      when brethren live together in unity!

2 It is like fine oil upon the head *
      that runs down upon the beard,

3 Upon the beard of Aaron, *
      and runs down upon the collar of his robe.

4 It is like the dew of Hermon *
      that falls upon the hills of Zion.

5 For there the LORD has ordained the blessing: *
      life for evermore.

139 *Domine, probasti*

1 LORD, you have searched me out and known me; *
      you know my sitting down and my rising up;

you discern my thoughts from afar.

2   You trace my journeys and my resting-places *
        and are acquainted with all my ways.

3   Indeed, there is not a word on my lips, *
        but you, O LORD, know it altogether.

4   You press upon me behind and before *
        and lay your hand upon me.

5   Such knowledge is too wonderful for me; *
        it is so high that I cannot attain to it.

6   Where can I go then from your Spirit? *
        where can I flee from your presence?

7   If I climb up to heaven, you are there; *
        if I make the grave my bed, you are there also.

8   If I take the wings of the morning *
        and dwell in the uttermost parts of the sea,

9   Even there your hand will lead me *
        and your right hand hold me fast.

10 If I say, "Surely the darkness will cover me, *
        and the light around me turn to night,"

11 Darkness is not dark to you;
    the night is as bright as the day; *
        darkness and light to you are both alike.

12 For you yourself created my inmost parts; *
        you knit me together in my mother's womb.

13 I will thank you because I am marvelously made; *
        your works are wonderful, and I know it well.

14 My body was not hidden from you, *
        while I was being made in secret
        and woven in the depths of the earth.

15 Your eyes beheld my limbs, yet unfinished in
            the womb;
    all of them were written in your book; *
        they were fashioned day by day,
        when as yet there was none of them.

16 How deep I find your thoughts, O God! *
        how great is the sum of them!

17 If I were to count them, they would be more
            in number than the sand; *
        to count them all, my life span would need to
            be like yours.

148 *Laudate Dominum*

1   Hallelujah!
    Praise the LORD from the heavens; *
        praise him in the heights.

2   Praise him, all you angels of his; *
        praise him, all his host.

3   Praise him, sun and moon; *
        praise him, all you shining stars.

4   Praise him, heaven of heavens, *
        and you waters above the heavens.

5   Let them praise the Name of the LORD; *
        for he commanded, and they were created.

6   He made them stand fast for ever and ever; *
        he gave them a law which shall not pass away.

7   Praise the LORD from the earth, *
        you sea-monsters and all deeps;

8   Fire and hail, snow and fog, *
        tempestuous wind, doing his will;

9   Mountains and all hills, *
        fruit trees and all cedars;

10   Wild beasts and all cattle, *
     creeping things and wingèd birds;

11   Kings of the earth and all peoples, *
     princes and all rulers of the world;

12   Young men and maidens, *
     old and young together.

13   Let them praise the Name of the LORD, *
     for his Name only is exalted,
     his splendor is over earth and heaven.

14   He has raised up strength for his people
   and praise for all his loyal servants, *
     the children of Israel, a people who are near him
     Hallelujah!

150   *Laudate Dominum*

1   Hallelujah!
Praise God in his holy temple; *
     praise him in the firmament of his power.

2   Praise him for his mighty acts; *
     praise him for his excellent greatness.

3 Praise him with the blast of the ram's-horn; *
    praise him with lyre and harp.

4 Praise him with timbrel and dance; *
    praise him with strings and pipe.

5 Praise him with resounding cymbals; *
    praise him with loud-clanging cymbals.

6 Let everything that has breath *
    praise the LORD.
    Hallelujah!

Canticles

Christ our Passover   *Pascha nostrum*

1 Corinthians 5:7–8; Romans 6:9–11; 1 Corinthians 15:20–22

Alleluia.
Christ our Passover has been sacrificed for us; *
    therefore let us keep the feast,
Not with the old leaven, the leaven of malice
        and evil, *
    but with the unleavened bread of sincerity
        and truth. Alleluia.

Christ being raised from the dead will never
     die again; *
  death no longer has dominion over him.
The death that he died, he died to sin, once for all; *
  but the life he lives, he lives to God.
So also consider yourselves dead to sin, *
  and alive to God in Jesus Christ our Lord.
     Alleluia.

Christ has been raised from the dead, *
  the first fruits of those who have fallen asleep.
For since by a man came death, *
  by a man has come also the resurrection of
     the dead.
For as in Adam all die, *
  so also in Christ shall all be made alive. Alleluia.

The First Song of Isaiah   *Ecce, Deus*

Isaiah 12:2–6

Surely, it is God who saves me; *
  I will trust in him and not be afraid.
For the Lord is my stronghold and my sure defense,
  and he will be my Savior.

Therefore you shall draw water with rejoicing *
      from the springs of salvation.
And on that day you shall say, *
      Give thanks to the Lord and call upon his Name;
Make his deeds known among the peoples; *
      see that they remember that his Name is exalted.
Sing the praises of the Lord, for he has done
            great things, *
      and this is known in all the world.
Cry aloud, inhabitants of Zion, ring out your joy, *
      for the great one in the midst of you is the
            Holy One of Israel.

Glory to the Father, and to the Son, and to
      the Holy Spirit: *
      as it was in the beginning, is now, and will be
            for ever. Amen.

The Song of the Redeemed   *Magna et mirabilia*

Revelation 15:3–4

O ruler of the universe, Lord God,
great deeds are they that you have done, *
      surpassing human understanding.

Your ways are ways of righteousness and truth, *
     O King of all the ages.

Who can fail to do you homage, Lord,
and sing the praises of your Name?
     for you only are the holy One.
All nations will draw near and fall down
          before you, *
     because your just and holy works have
          been revealed.

Glory to the Father, and to the Son, and to
          the Holy Spirit: *
     as it was in the beginning, is now, and will be
          for ever. Amen.

Glory to God   *Gloria in excelsis*

Glory to God in the highest,
     and peace to his people on earth.

Lord God, heavenly King,
almighty God and Father,
     we worship you, we give you thanks,
     we praise you for your glory.

Lord Jesus Christ, only Son of the Father,
Lord God, Lamb of God,
you take away the sin of the world:
    have mercy on us;
you are seated at the right hand of the Father:
    receive our prayer.

For you alone are the Holy One,
you alone are the Lord,
you alone are the Most High,
    Jesus Christ,
    with the Holy Spirit,
    in the glory of God the Father. Amen.

The Song of Mary   *Magnificat*

Luke 1:46–55

My soul doth magnify the Lord, *
    and my spirit hath rejoiced in God my Savior.
For he hath regarded *
    the lowliness of his handmaiden.
For behold from henceforth *
    all generations shall call me blessed.
For he that is mighty hath magnified me, *
    and holy is his Name.

And his mercy is on them that fear him *
  throughout all generations.
He hath showed strength with his arm; *
  he hath scattered the proud in the imagination
    of their hearts.
He hath put down the mighty from their seat, *
  and hath exalted the humble and meek.
He hath filled the hungry with good things, *
  and the rich he hath sent empty away.
He remembering his mercy hath holpen his
    servant Israel, *
  as he promised to our forefathers,
  Abraham and his seed for ever.

Glory to the Father, and to the Son, and to
    the Holy Spirit: *
  as it was in the beginning, is now, and will be
    for ever. Amen.

The Song of Simeon   *Nunc dimittis*

Luke 2:29–32

Lord, now lettest thou thy servant depart in peace,
  according to thy word;

For mine eyes have seen thy salvation, *
    which thou hast prepared before the face
        of all people,
To be a light to lighten the Gentiles, *
    and to be the glory of thy people Israel.

Glory to the Father, and to the Son, and to
        the Holy Spirit: *
    as it was in the beginning, is now, and will be
        for ever. Amen.

Bible Readings

Selected Bible Readings

Readings

The Ten Commandments
Exodus 20:1–17

And God spoke all these words, saying, "I am the Lord your God, who brought you out of the land of Egypt, out of the house of bondage. You shall have no other gods before me. You shall not make for yourself a graven image, or any likeness of anything that is in heaven above, or that is in the earth beneath, or that is in the water under the earth; you shall not bow down to them or serve them; for I the Lord your God am a jealous God, visiting the iniquity of the fathers upon the children to the third and the fourth generation of those who hate me, but showing steadfast love to thousands of those who love me and keep my commandments. You shall not take the name of the Lord your God in vain; for the Lord will not hold him guiltless who takes his name in vain. Remember the sabbath day, to keep it holy. Six days you shall labor, and do all your work; but the seventh day is a sabbath to the Lord your God; in it you shall not do any work, you, or your son, or your daughter, your manservant, or your maidservant, or your cattle, or the sojourner who is within your gates; for in six days the Lord made heaven and earth, the sea, and all that is in them, and rested the seventh day; therefore the Lord blessed the sabbath day and hallowed it. Honor your father and your mother, that your days may be long in the land which the Lord your God gives you. You shall not kill. You shall not commit adultery. You shall not steal. You shall not bear false witness against your neighbor. You shall not covet your neighbor's house; you shall not covet your neighbor's wife, or his manservant, or his maidservant, or his ox, or his ass, or anything that is your neighbor's."

Prophecy of the Coming of Christ

Isaiah 11:1–10

There shall come forth a shoot from the stump of Jesse, and a branch shall grow out of his roots. And the Spirit of the Lord shall rest upon him, the spirit of wisdom and understanding, the spirit of counsel and might, the spirit of knowledge and the fear of the Lord. And his delight shall be in the fear of the Lord. He shall not judge by what his eyes see, or decide by what his ears hear; but with righteousness he shall judge the poor, and decide with equity for the meek of the earth; and he shall smite the earth with the rod of his mouth, and with the breath of his lips he shall slay the wicked. Righteousness shall be the girdle of his waist, and faithfulness the girdle of his loins. The wolf shall dwell with the lamb, and the leopard shall lie down with the kid, and the calf and the lion and the fatling together, and a little child shall lead them. The cow and the bear shall feed; their young shall lie down together; and the lion shall eat straw like the ox. The sucking child shall play over the hole of the asp, and the weaned child shall put his hand on the adder's den. They shall not hurt or destroy in all my holy mountain; for the earth shall be full of the knowledge of the Lord as the waters cover the sea. In that day the root of Jesse shall stand as an ensign to the peoples; him shall the nations seek, and his dwellings shall be glorious.

News of the Returning Exiles

Isaiah 40:1–11

Comfort, comfort my people, says your God. Speak tenderly to Jerusalem, and cry to her that her warfare is ended, that her iniquity is pardoned, that she has received from the Lord's hand double for all her sins. A voice cries: "In the wilderness prepare the way of the Lord, make straight in the desert a highway for our God. Every valley shall be lifted up, and every mountain and hill be made low; the uneven ground shall become level, and the rough places a plain. And the glory of the Lord shall be revealed, and all flesh shall see it together, for the mouth of the Lord has spoken." A voice says, "Cry!" And I said, "What shall I cry?" All flesh is grass, and all its beauty is like the flower of the field. The grass withers, the flower fades, when the breath of the Lord blows upon it; surely the people is grass. The grass withers, the flower fades; but the word of our God will stand for ever. Get you up to a high mountain, O Zion, herald of good tidings; lift up your voice with strength, O Jerusalem, herald of good tidings, lift it up, fear not; say to the cities of Judah, "Behold your God!" Behold, the Lord God comes with might, and his arm rules for him; behold, his reward is with him; and his recompense before him. He will feed his flock like a shepherd, he will gather the lambs in his arms, he will carry them in his bosom, and gently lead those that are with young.

Prophecy of the New Covenant

Jeremiah 31:31–34

Behold, the days are coming, says the Lord, when I will make a new covenant with the house of Israel and the house of Judah, not like the covenant which I made with their fathers when I took them by the hand to bring them out of the land of Egypt, my covenant which they broke, though I was their husband, says the Lord.

But this is the covenant which I will make with the house of Israel after those days, says the Lord: I will put my law within them, and I will write it upon their hearts; and I will be their God, and they shall be my people. And no longer shall each man teach his neighbor and each his brother, saying, 'Know the Lord,' for they shall all know me from the least of them to the greatest, says the Lord; for I will forgive their iniquity, and I will remember their sin no more.

The Annunciation

St. Luke 1:26–38

In the sixth month the angel Gabriel was sent from God to a city of Galilee named Nazareth, to a virgin betrothed to a man whose name was

Joseph, of the house of David; and the virgin's name was Mary. And he came to her and said, "Hail, O favored one, the Lord is with you!" But she was greatly troubled at the saying, and considered in her mind what sort of greeting this might be. And the angel said to her, "Do not be afraid, Mary, for you have found favor with God. And behold, you will conceive in your womb and bear a son, and you shall call his name Jesus. He will be great, and will be called the Son of the Most High; and the Lord God will give to him the throne of his father David, and he will reign over the house of Jacob for ever; and of his kingdom there will be no end." And Mary said to the angel, "How shall this be, since I have no husband?" And the angel said to her, "The Holy Spirit will come upon you, and the power of the Most High will overshadow you; therefore the child to be born will be called holy, the Son of God. And behold, your kinswoman Elizabeth in her old age has also conceived a son; and this is the sixth month with her who was called barren. For with God nothing will be impossible." And Mary said,

"Behold, I am the handmaid of the Lord; let it be to me according to your word." And the angel departed from her.

The Birth of Jesus
St. Luke 2:1–20

In those days a decree went out from Caesar Augustus that all the world should be enrolled. This was the first enrollment, when Quirinius was governor of Syria. And all went to be enrolled, each to his own city. And Joseph also went up from Galilee, from the city of Nazareth, to Judea, to the city of David, which is called Bethlehem, because he was of the house and lineage of David, to be enrolled with Mary, his betrothed, who was with child. And while they were there, the time came for her to be delivered. And she gave birth to her first-born son and wrapped him in swaddling cloths, and laid him in a manger, because there was no place for them in the inn. And in that region there were shepherds out in the field, keeping watch over their flock by night. And an angel of the Lord appeared to them, and the glory of the Lord shone around them, and they were filled with fear. And the angel said to them, "Be not afraid; for behold, I bring you good news of a great joy which will come to all the people; for to you is born this day in the city of David a Savior, who is Christ the Lord. And this will be a sign for you: you will find a babe wrapped in swaddling cloths and lying in a manger." And suddenly there was with the angel a multitude of the heavenly host praising God and saying, "Glory to God in the highest, and on earth peace among men with whom he is pleased!" When the angels went away from them into heaven, the shepherds said to one another, "Let us go over to Bethlehem and see this thing that has happened, which the Lord has made known to us." And they went with haste, and found Mary and Joseph, and the babe lying in a manger. And when they said it they made known the saying which had been told them concerning this child; and all who heard it wondered at what the shepherds told them. But Mary kept all these things, pondering them in her heart.

And the shepherds returned, glorifying and praising God for all they had heard and seen, as it had been told them.

The Prologue

St. John 1:1–14

In the beginning was the Word, and the Word was with God, and the Word was God. He was in the beginning with God; all things were made through him, and without him was not anything made that was made. In him was life, and the life was the light of men. The light shines in the darkness, and the darkness has not overcome it. There was a man sent from God, whose name was John. He came for testimony, to bear witness to the light, that all might believe through him. He was not the light, but came to bear witness to the light. The true light that enlightens every man was coming into the world. He was in the world, and the world was made through him, yet the world knew him not. He came to his own home, and his own people received him not. But to all who received him, who believed in his name, he gave power to become children of God; who were born, not of blood nor of the will of the flesh nor of the will of man, but of God. And the Word became flesh and dwelt among us, full of grace and truth; we have beheld his glory, glory as of the only Son from the Father.

The Baptism of Jesus
St. Mark 1:2–13

As it is written in Isaiah the prophet, "Behold, I send my messenger before thy face, who shall prepare thy way; the voice of one crying in the wilderness: Prepare the way of the Lord, make his paths straight—" John the baptizer appeared in the wilderness, preaching a baptism of repentance for the forgiveness of sins. And there went out to him all the country of Judea, and all the people of Jerusalem; and they were baptized by him in the river Jordan, confessing their sins. Now John was clothed with camel's hair, and had a leather girdle around his waist, and ate locusts and wild honey. And he preached, saying, "After me comes he who is mightier than I, the thong of whose sandals I am not worthy to stoop down and untie. I have baptized you with water; but he will baptize you with the Holy Spirit." In those days Jesus came from Nazareth of Galilee and was baptized by John in the Jordan. And when he came up out of the water, immediately he saw the heavens opened and the Spirit descending upon him like a dove; and a voice came from heaven, "Thou art my beloved Son; with thee I am well pleased." The Spirit immediately drove him out into the wilderness. And he was in the wilderness forty days, tempted by Satan; and he was with the wild beasts; and the angels ministered to him.

The Beatitudes

St. Matthew 5:1–12

Seeing the crowds, he went up on the mountain, and when he sat down his disciples came to him. And he opened his mouth and taught them, saying: "Blessed are the poor in spirit, for theirs is the kingdom of heaven. Blessed are those who mourn, for they shall be comforted. Blessed are the meek, for they shall inherit the earth. Blessed are those who hunger and thirst for righteousness, for they shall be satisfied. Blessed are the merciful, for they shall obtain mercy. Blessed are the pure in heart, for they shall see God. Blessed are the peacemakers, for they shall be called sons of God. Blessed are those who are persecuted for righteousness' sake, for theirs is the kingdom of heaven. Blessed are you when men revile you and persecute you and utter all kinds of evil against you falsely on my account. Rejoice and be glad, for your reward is great in heaven, for so men persecuted the prophets who were before you."

The Names of and Charge to the Disciples

St. Matthew 10:1–15

And he called to him his twelve disciples and gave them authority over unclean spirits, to cast them out, and to heal every disease and every infirmity. The names of the twelve apostles are these: first, Simon, who is called Peter, and Andrew his brother; James the son of Zebedee, and John his brother; Philip and Bartholomew; Thomas and Matthew the tax collector; James the son of Alphaeus, and Thaddaeus; Simon the Cananaean, and Judas Iscariot, who betrayed him. These twelve Jesus sent out, charging them, "Go nowhere among the Gentiles, and enter no town of the Samaritans, but go rather to the lost sheep of the house of Israel. And preach as you go, saying, 'The kingdom of heaven is at hand.' Heal the sick, raise the dead, cleanse lepers, cast out demons. You received without paying, give without pay. Take no gold, nor silver, nor copper in your belts, no bag for your journey, nor two tunics, nor sandals, nor a staff; for the laborer deserves his food. And whatever town or village you enter, find out who is worthy in it, and stay with him until you depart. As you enter the house, salute it. And if the house is worthy, let your peace come upon it; but if it is not worthy, let your peace return to you. And if any one will not receive you or listen to your words, shake off the dust from your feet as you leave that house or town. Truly, I say to you, it shall be more tolerable on the day of judgment for the land of Sodom and Gomorrah than for that town.

The Vine and the Branches

St. John 15:1–17

"I am the true vine, and my Father is the vine-dresser. Every branch of mine that bears no fruit, he takes away, and every branch that does bear fruit he prunes, that it may bear more fruit. You are already made clean by the word which I have spoken to you. Abide in me, and I in you. As the branch cannot bear fruit by itself, unless it abides in the vine, neither can you, unless you abide in me. I am the vine, you are the branches. He who abides in me, and I in him, he it is that bears much fruit, for apart from me you can do nothing. If a man does not abide in me, he is cast forth as a branch and withers; and the branches are gathered, thrown into the fire and burned. If you abide in me, and my words abide in you, ask whatever you will, and it shall be done for you. By this my Father is glorified, that you bear much fruit, and so prove to be my disciples. As the Father has loved me, so have I loved you; abide in my love. If you keep my commandments, you will abide in my love, just as I have kept my Father's commandments and abide in his love. These things I have spoken to you, that my joy may be in you, and that your joy may be full. This is my commandment, that you love one another as I have loved you. Greater love has no man than this, that a man lay down his life for his friends. You are my friends if you do what I command you. No longer do I call you servants, for the servant does not know what his master is doing; but I have called you friends, for all that I have heard from my Father I have made known to you. You did not choose me, but I chose you and appointed you that you should go and bear fruit and that your fruit should abide; so that whatever you ask the Father in my name, he may give it to you. This I command you, to love one another."

Sacrifice

St. Mark 10:17–31

And as he was setting out on his journey, a man ran up and knelt before him, and asked him, "Good Teacher, what must I do to inherit eternal life?" And Jesus said to him, "Why do you call me good? No one is good but God alone. You know the commandments: 'Do not kill, Do not commit adultery, Do not steal, Do not bear false witness, Do not defraud, Honor your father and mother.'" And he said to him, "Teacher, all these I have observed from my youth." And Jesus looking upon him loved him, and said to him, "You lack one thing; go, sell what you have, and give to the poor, and you will have treasure in heaven; and come, follow me." At that saying his countenance fell, and he went away sorrowful; for he had great possessions. And Jesus looked around and said to his disciples, "How hard it will be for those who have riches to enter the kingdom of God!" And the disciples were amazed at his words. But Jesus said to them again, "Children, how hard it is to enter the kingdom of God! It is easier for a camel to go through the eye of a needle than for a rich man to enter the kingdom of God." And they were exceedingly astonished, and said to him, "Then who can be saved?" Jesus looked at them and said, "With men it is impossible, but not with God; for all things are possible with God." Peter began to say to him, "Lo, we have left everything and followed you." Jesus said, "Truly, I say to you, there is no one who has left house or brothers or sisters or mother or father or children or lands, for my sake and for the gospel, who will not receive a hundred-fold now in this time, houses and brothers and sisters and mothers and children and lands, with persecutions, and in the age to come eternal life. But many that are first will be last, and the last first."

The Feeding of the Five Thousand
St. John 6:1–13

After this Jesus went to the other side of the Sea of Galilee, which is the Sea of Tiberias. And a multitude followed him, because they saw the signs which he did on those who were diseased. Jesus went up on the mountain, and there sat down with his disciples. Now the Passover, the feast of the Jews, was at hand. Lifting up his eyes, then, and seeing that a multitude was coming to him, Jesus said to Philip, "How are we to buy bread, so that these people may eat?" This he said to test him, for he himself knew what he would do. Philip answered him, "Two hundred denarii would not buy enough bread for each of them to get a little." One of his disciples, Andrew, Simon Peter's brother, said to him, "There is a lad here who has five barley loaves and two fish; but what are they among so many?" Jesus said, "Make the people sit down." Now there was much grass in the place; so the men sat down, in number about five thousand. Jesus then took the loaves, and when he had given thanks, he distributed them to those who were seated; so also the fish, as much as they wanted. And when they had eaten their fill, he told his disciples, "Gather up the fragments left over, that nothing may be lost." So they gathered them up and filled twelve baskets with fragments from the five barley loaves, left by those who had eaten.

Palm Sunday

St. Matthew 21:1–11

And when they drew near to Jerusalem and came to Bethpage, to the Mount of Olives, then Jesus sent two disciples, saying to them, "Go into the village opposite you, and immediately you will find an ass tied, and a colt with her; untie them and bring them to me. If any one says anything to you, you shall say, 'The Lord has need of them,' and he will send them immediately." This took place to fulfill what was spoken by the prophet, saying, "Tell the daughter of Zion, Behold, your king is coming to you, humble, and mounted on an ass, and on a colt, the foul of an ass." The disciples went and did as Jesus had directed them; they brought the ass and the colt, and put their garments on them, and he sat thereon. Most of the crowd spread their garments on the road, and others cut branches from the trees and spread them on the road. And the crowds that went before him and that followed him shouted, "Hosanna to the Son of David! Blessed is he who comes in the name of the Lord! Hosanna in the highest!" And when he entered Jerusalem, all the city was stirred, saying, "Who is this?" And the crowds said, "This is the prophet Jesus from Nazareth of Galilee."

The Last Supper

St. Matthew 26:26–30

Now as they were eating, Jesus took bread, and blessed, and broke it, and gave it to the disciples and said, "Take, eat; this is my body." And he took a cup, and when he had given thanks he gave it to them, saying, "Drink of it, all of you; for this is my blood of the covenant, which is poured out for many for the forgiveness of sins. I tell you I shall not drink again of this fruit of the vine until that day when I drink it new with you in my Father's kingdom." And when they had sung a hymn, they went out to the Mount of Olives.

Easter

St. Luke 24:36b–53

Jesus himself stood among them. But they were startled and frightened, and supposed that they saw a spirit. And he said to them, "Why are you troubled, and why do questionings rise in your hearts? See my hands and my feet, that it is I myself; handle me, and see; for a spirit has not flesh and bones as you see that I have." And while they still disbelieved for joy, and wondered, he said to them, "Have you anything here to eat?" They gave him a piece of broiled fish, and he took it and ate before them. Then he said to them, "These are my words which I spoke to you, while I was still with you, that everything written about me in the law of Moses and the prophets and the psalms must be fulfilled." Then he opened their minds to understand the scriptures, and said to them, "Thus it is written, that the Christ should suffer and on the third day rise from the dead, and that repentance and forgiveness of sins should be preached in his name to all nations, beginning from Jerusalem. You are witnesses of these things. And behold, I send the promise of my Father upon you; but stay in the city, until you are clothed with power from on high." Then he led them out as far as Bethany, and lifting up his hands he blessed them. While he blessed them, he parted from them, and was carried up into heaven. And they returned to Jerusalem with great joy, and were continually in the temple blessing God.

The Mission to the World

St. Matthew 28:16–20

Now the eleven disciples went to Galilee, to the mountain to which Jesus had directed them. And when they saw him they worshiped him; but some doubted. And Jesus came and said to them, "All authority in heaven and on earth has been given to me. Go therefore and make disciples of all nations, baptizing them in the name of the Father and of the Son and of the Holy Spirit, teaching them to observe all that I have commanded you; and lo, I am with you always, to the close of the age."

Faith Guarantees Salvation
Romans 5:1–5

Therefore, since we are justified by faith, we have peace with God through our Lord Jesus Christ. Through him we have obtained access to his grace in which we stand, and we rejoice in our hope of sharing the glory of God. More than that, we rejoice in our sufferings, knowing that suffering produces endurance, and endurance produces character, and character produces hope, and hope does not disappoint us, because God's love has been poured into our hearts through the Holy Spirit which has been given to us.

The Christian's Spiritual Life
Romans 8:14–19, 34–35, 37–39

For all who are led by the Spirit of God are sons of God. For you did not receive the spirit of slavery to fall back into fear, but you have received the spirit of sonship. When we cry, "Abba! Father!" it is the Spirit himself bearing witness with our spirit that we are children of God, and if children, then heirs, heirs of God and fellow heirs with Christ, provided we suffer with him in order that we may also be glorified with him. I consider that the sufferings of this present time are not worth comparing with the glory that is to be revealed to us. For the creation waits with eager longing for the revealing of the sons of God. Who is to condemn? Is it Christ Jesus, who died, yes, who was raised from the dead, who is at the right hand of God, who indeed intercedes for us? Who shall separate us from the love of Christ? Shall tribulation, or distress, or persecution, or famine, or nakedness, or peril, or sword? No, in all these things we are more than conquerors through him who loved us. For I am sure that neither death, nor life, nor angels, nor principalities, nor things present, nor things to come, nor powers, nor height, nor depth, nor anything else in all creation, will be able to separate us from the love of God in Christ Jesus our Lord.

Christ the Power
and the Wisdom of God

1 Corinthians 1:23–25

We preach Christ crucified, a stumbling block
to Jews and folly to Gentiles, but to those who
are called, both Jews and Greeks, Christ the
power of God and the wisdom of God. For the
foolishness of God is wiser than men, and the
weakness of God is stronger than men.

The Apostolate in Action

2 Corinthians 5:17–21

Therefore, if anyone is in Christ, he is a new
creation; the old has passed away, behold, the
new has come. All this is from God, who
through Christ reconciled us to himself and
gave us the ministry of reconciliation; that is, in
Christ God was reconciling the world to himself, not counting their trespasses against them,
and entrusting to us the message of reconciliation. So we are ambassadors for Christ, God
making his appeal through us. We beseech you

on behalf of Christ, be reconciled to God. For our sake he made him to be sin who knew no sin, so that in him we might become the righteousness of God.